I Will Be
FREE

My Declaration to Continual Self-Deliverance

NATALIE NICHOLE

I Will Be
FREE

Published by Krystal Lee Enterprises (KLE Publishing)
Copyright © 2024 by Natalie Washington. All rights reserved. Please send comments and questions:
Krystal Lee Enterprises
770-240-0089 Ext. 1
sales@KLEPub.com

To Reach the Author:
Email: lovethatsavesyou@gmail.com
Web: Lovethatsaves.com
Social: Facebook Page: Love that Saves

Printed in the United States of America.
All rights reserved. No part of this book may be reproduced or transmitted in any form or by any means, electronic or mechanical, including photocopying, recording, or any information storage and retrieval system without written permission of the publisher except for brief quotations used in reviews, written specifically for inclusion in a newspaper, blog, magazine, or academic paper.

ISBN: 978-1-945066-63-4

I want to express my heartfelt gratitude to Jesus for guiding me in the completion of this work.

To my amazing husband, Bobby: thank you for always listening to my thoughts, both on and off the page. Your unwavering love and support mean the world to me.

My family has been my greatest motivation. I appreciate the lessons learned and the love that drives me to become better.

A special thank you to my Pastors, Dr. Steven and JoAnn Thompson. Everything I know about ministry comes from you. Thank you for planting the seeds and allowing me the time to grow.

I appreciate the heartfelt foreword written by Lady Keana Thompson. I love you and am so thankful for ministry of you and Pastor Stephen Thompson.

To my Live Again Community: your support is invaluable. Though there are too many to name, I appreciate every prayer, word of encouragement, and God-inspired idea that has helped Love That Saves flourish. Thank you for enabling me and others to truly Live Again.

Pray Again, Love Again, Live Again

Natalie Washington

Greetings!

Given honor to God and his Son, Jesus Christ. I thank God for abiding in me and me abiding in Him! I always had a relationship with the Lord, but I was in a low place at one point in my life. I didn't know what to do or where to turn, but I was searching for God. Live Again Ministries blessed my life in so many ways that I cannot tell it all.

It helped me find ME first and foremost by sacrificing my extra time and dedicating it to spending more time with God rather than on things that are not so much of Him. It challenged me to pray more, to look at myself first, and to forgive not just myself but others as well. In doing so, my family came back together, broken relationships were mended and healed, and for that, I gained a new level of maturity and wisdom through Christ!

Pray Again (Luke 18:1) 🖤 Love Again (1 John 4:16) 🖤 Live Again (John 3:16) 🖤 will always be my affirmation and daily reminder because it is God's word!

Love,

~ Alicia N. Garrett~
Be Bold, Be Beautiful, Be You

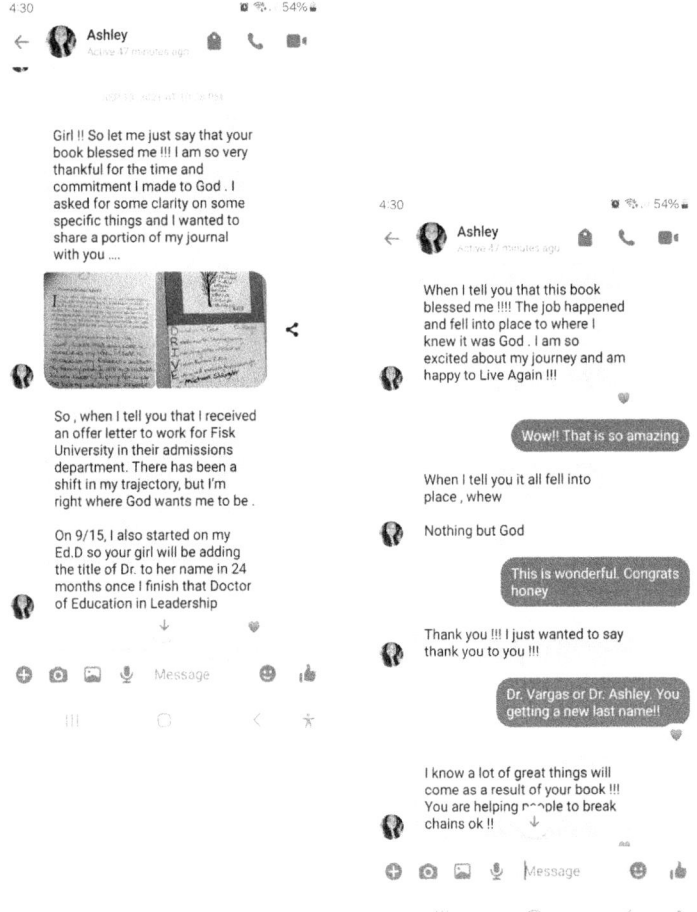

> Girl !! So let me just say that your book blessed me !!! I am so very thankful for the time and commitment I made to God. I asked for some clarity on some specific things and I wanted to share a portion of my journal with you ....
>
> So, when I tell you that I received an offer letter to work for Fisk University in their admissions department. There has been a shift in my trajectory, but I'm right where God wants me to be.
>
> On 9/15, I also started on my Ed.D so your girl will be adding the title of Dr. to her name in 24 months once I finish that Doctor of Education in Leadership
>
> When I tell you that this book blessed me !!!! The job happened and fell into place to where I knew it was God. I am so excited about my journey and am happy to Live Again !!!

Wow!! That is so amazing

> When I tell you it all fell into place, whew
>
> Nothing but God

This is wonderful. Congrats honey

> Thank you !!! I just wanted to say thank you to you !!!

Dr. Vargas or Dr. Ashley. You getting a new last name!!

> I know a lot of great things will come as a result of your book !!! You are helping people to break chains ok !!

Dr. Ashley Dantzler

Nat,

Please see below and understand this testimony doesn't give my true experience justice.

I wanted to take this moment to express the incredible impact that the recent experience with Live Again has had on me. The words shared during this time served as a powerful reminder of the endless blessings and transformations that God brings into our lives.

Witnessing the beautiful journey of faith you have with God fills my heart with joy and gratitude. Being physically present at the Live Again convention allowed me to truly witness the sanctifying power of God in action. His presence was so tangible, reminding me of my purpose and identity in Him.

The experience was nothing short of a spiritual awakening, a moment where I felt truly born again. It rejuvenated my spirit, reignited my faith, and inspired me to keep pressing on, eager to see what wonderful blessings the future holds.

Thank you for being a shining example of faith and love. Your journey has touched my heart in ways I can't even begin to describe. May we continue to walk in God's light and grace, knowing that He is always by our side, guiding us every step of the way.

With love and blessings,
Nicole J

The first time I read Live Again written by Natalie Nichole I had just returned from vacation and found my self at a low point in my life. I had fell, I felt lost, and didn't know how to pick up the pieces to my life or my relationship with God. I was seeking God and looking for my true self. I was also looking for tangible tools to help me put things in perspective and provide some light in my dark place. I desperately needed practical tools to help me pick up the broken pieces of my life. Live Again helped me do just that.

For 21 days I was able to concentrate and use this devotional to help me reposition myself under the shadow of the almighty God, I found courage, strength, and power to get back up and Live Again. I was able to regain a new outlook on my purpose and rekindle the fire I had for the Will of God over my life. I am very thankful to the 21 day devotional Live Again and its Author Natalie Nichole for being transparent, practical, and truly a blessing to me in my darkest hour. This book truly did help me to know that I too could Live Again.

Thank you,
Brittany Riley

Foreword

I am deeply honored to write this foreword. Having witnessed the growth and journey of Min. Natalie firsthand, I can say that her evolution has been nothing short of inspiring. Both of us have navigated challenging paths, and through the grace and mercy of God, we've overcome these hurdles. It's clear to me that the ministry that has emerged has always been a part of Min. Natalie.

I am incredibly excited about this new book. Reflecting on her previous work, "Live Again," I realized I embarked on a journey I didn't know I needed. Each day presented a new lesson that was essential for me. I have long understood that fasting and prayer are vital to accessing God's power, but this book provided me with what felt like a "Road Map" to deliverance.

We all need deliverance from something or someone, and for me, it was deliverance from my own self-sabotage. Although I had been working on my mental well-being, I realized I was falling short spiritually. My daily prayers and scripture readings, though meaningful, were not enough for the spiritual growth I sought.

Many people need to understand that one can possess a gift without fully utilizing it according to God's will. "Live Again" was instrumental in addressing this. Min. Natalie's words spoke to the young girl in me who lacked nurturing, to the 18-year-old who never imagined pursuing a college education, and to the person who needed to refocus her priorities on God. This book reignited my spirit and brought clarity to someone who had felt lost for a long time.

Her latest work represents a new step in this journey. Deliverance is an ongoing process, and with each victory comes new challenges. Even when faced with setbacks, the key is to rise and continue striving until we succeed. Life's challenges can be daunting, but this book equips us with the tools to overcome them. Remember, a setback is just another opportunity to persevere.

I felt led to let God guide my words for this foreword. This book deserves an original introduction befitting the thoughtful, loving, and dedicated author it represents. Min. Natalie embodies the principles she writes about, and her personal experiences enrich her message. I pray that her work blesses you as much as it has blessed me and that she is abundantly rewarded for sharing her heart and allowing God's Word and Spirit to flow through her.

Enjoy this book and cherish its message.
Blessings and much love,

Lady Keana Thompson, MSW, LSW
God's Grace Community Church, Indianapolis

Table of Contents

INTRODUCTION	13
BEFORE YOU BEGIN	17
PRAYER FOR HEALTHY RELATIONSHIPS	24
PRAYER FOR THE READER	25
I WILL BE FREE FROM REJECTION	27
I WILL BE FREE FROM FEAR	33
I WILL BE FREE FROM SELF-SABOTAGE	39
I WILL BE FREE FROM UNFORGIVENESS	45
I WILL BE FREE FROM RESISTANCE	51
I WILL BE FREE FROM ANGER	57
I WILL BE FREE FROM ACCUSATION	63
I WILL BE FREE FROM CONFUSION & CHAOS	69
I WILL BE FREE FROM GRIEF	75
I WILL BE FREE FROM IRRESPONSIBLE STEWARDSHIP	81
I WILL BE FREE FROM SEXUAL SINS	87

I WILL BE FREE FROM SHAME	95
I WILL BE FREE FROM BITTERNESS	101
I WILL BE FREE FROM NEGATIVE WORDS	107
I WILL BE FREE FROM PRIDE	113
I WILL BE FREE FROM BROKEN HEART	119
I WILL BE FREE FROM THE BONDAGE OF SICKNESS, DISEASE, AND INFIRMITY	125
I WILL BE FREE FROM DISTRACTIONS	131
I WILL BE FREE FROM IMPATIENCE	137
I WILL BE FREE FROM LAZINESS	143
I WILL BE FREE FROM ME	149
NEXT STEPS!	155
ABOUT THE AUTHOR	159

YOU WILL BE FREE

Introduction

Introduction

Thank you for joining Love That Saves on another journey to #liveagain.

The I Will Be Free Challenge is a 21-day topical prayer devotional that focuses on continual self-deliverance. As a believer in Christ, you may have heard someone say that Christ wants you to be free. But you may not understand the secret formula to obtaining freedom. Well, I will help you solve that mystery today. The secret formula to walking in freedom gifted to us from Christ is being intentional about your walk with Christ.

Yes, it's simple, but not always so simple. Walking with Christ requires intentionality and ongoing discipline. As mentioned earlier in this book, deliverance is not only received at isolated events such as the altar, church, conferences, etc. Deliverance occurs when you make an intentional decision to live disciplined in Christ by actively applying the truth of God's Word to your heart and actions ***CONSISTENTLY.***

The secret formula of deliverance looks like this:

$$\frac{\textit{Christ} \, (\textbf{discipline} + \textbf{intentionality})}{\textit{Time}}$$

Deliverance only happens when we surrender our thoughts and actions to Christ. Christ is the constant variable in our lives and never changes. Instead, He multiplies himself in

Introduction

our lives. As you find yourselves searching for freedom in people, places, things, and systems, I want to remind you to surrender your thoughts on deliverance and allow God to teach you His principles that will yield an abundance of fruit in your life.

This surrender starts with intentional discipline. Over time, you will see results and experience new freedom in Christ.

"Stand fast therefore in the liberty wherewith Christ hath made us free, and be not entangled again with the yoke of bondage." Galatians 5:1

Each day, you will read a focal scripture and Psalm. The Psalm can be used as a personal prayer and praise to God. Please refer to the daily checklist to complete this challenge effectively. If you desire to add a fast, please refer to Live Again by Natalie Nichole on Amazon for fasting tips and suggestions.

LIVE AGAIN: Putting Broken Hearts Back Together Again
https://a.co/d/9UnGhNk

Needs
- Journal
- Bible or Bible App
- Desire to take daily steps towards creating new disciplines
- Read daily scriptures to include a daily Psalm for prayer points
- Make this personal
- Consider reading different versions such as the Message, Amplified, English Standard Version, New Living Translation, and God's Word for easier understanding.
- Write down scriptures and personal prayers

- Use daily checklist

Daily Checklist
- Read/study God's Word
- Repent
- Request God's Help
- Receive God's Love, Correction, and Instruction
- Re-Envision Yourself Free
- Remind yourself of God's Word and promises to you

Additional Resources

Join The Live Again Facebook Community

Subscribe to Live Again YouTube

Listen to the I Will Be Free Audio Recordings on YouTube @LiveAgain21
01/11-2024-01/31-2024
Purchase Live Again 21-Day Prayer and Fasting Devotional

Before You Begin

Before You Begin

Call to Deliverance

The Why

Whom the Son Has Set Free is Free Indeed John 8:36
God reveals to heal it.

Deliverance can seem like a taunting task or even scary because of things you may have seen or heard, especially if you have watched any movies that require an exorcism. Trust me, this book is not about teaching you how to cast out demons. It will teach you how to tell yourself no and become more disciplined in your thoughts and actions. God uses deliverance in the lives of believers in Christ to further heal issues at the root cause.

Anything that God reveals to you is for you to accept a new level of healing. So, please don't be intimidated by the word deliverance. This is merely your decision to live a life that God is pleased with. I want to encourage you that deliverance is a lifestyle. It can not be an individual isolated event. Instead, it must be an accumulation of times and seasons in your life that are submitted to Christ.

You may have heard the saying, "life be lifing". This means things will continue to happen in our lives without our approval. This is why we must build an urgency as believers to remain rooted in the principles of Christ and to seek Him first for help. If not, life will have you drift

Before You Begin

into a wilderness of despair. This is why deliverance cannot be an isolated event or something that happens at the beginning or end of the year.

The good news is deliverance is for you and the children's bread (Mark 7:27). Deliverance is necessary and ongoing. As long as you are breathing, there will always be a need for deliverance because life sometimes weighs on us. Jesus wants us to give Him our burdens because His yoke is easy and His burden is light (Matthew 11:28-30).

But sometimes, the exchange is not an easy process, and we have to be taught how to give the things that hurt us to Christ. This starts with a decision to be intentional. We have to consistently find time to learn God's word, apply His principles, and allow our faith to grow differently in every season of our lives.

I want you to approach deliverance with realistic goals in mind. The first is that there will be days when you don't get it quite right. Two is that there may be several days when you feel like life is overwhelming and not fair at all. Deliverance has to be a conscious decision to live disciplined for Christ daily. Submitting to live delivered means you allow the Word of God to transform you, and you will not be condemned by your moral failures (which we all have).

As we live disciplined for Christ, we have the potential to lessen the devastating consequences that come as a result of undisciplined decisions and actions. The I Will Be Free devotion encourages you to live more committed to Christ daily. Christ wants you to experience His freedom in your lifetime so that you can teach others about His goodness.

I pray that today is the day you live more committed to Christ and choose to discipline yourself for ongoing deliverance. Say it with me: I WILL BE FREE!!

Note to Readers
August 14th 2024

I am sitting on my porch, attempting to write a letter to you. I pray that reading this small snippet of I Will Be Free will encourage you to initiate the posture of freedom in your life now. Freedom is not based on your ability to define it. Freedom in Christ comes from your wants aligning with God's will for your life. Have you ever prayed for something, and it came to pass exactly the way you wanted it to?

When that happens, you can begin to think that God answers all your prayers because you prayed powerfully, are faithful (so you think), and have all kinds of favor on your life. But what happens when God doesn't answer the prayer exactly as you wanted? Does that mean you are not powerful, faithful, or favored?

Not exactly. See, there are many things we can be certain about, but there are things that only God knows. We have to really trust that even when God doesn't answer our prayers, He still loves us. You are still saved, bought with a price on Calvary's Cross. The penalty for your sins has been revoked, and you still have freedom in Christ.

Background: in 2008, I was diagnosed with an incurable kidney disease called focal segmental glomerulo-

Before You Begin

sclerosis (FSGS). I am not a medical doctor and trust me, I have difficulty pronouncing this. This disease is considered incurable. At the time, I was in really bad shape and was told I would be on dialysis in 3 years. Over several years, doctor visits, lab draws, medical study, and a plethora of medications, the doctor deemed me healed. I am a walking miracle, stable and in remission without dialysis.

Well, fast forward. Covid came on the scene, and after catching it a few times, I started to have some problems. My kidneys were impacted, and my stable kidney function began to drop to approximately 40%. The goal was to do all I could to prolong my kidney function, exercise, lose weight, improve my diet, and, by all means, don't get sick, especially with COVID-19.

8/14/2024 I tested positive with Covid for the 3rd time. Up to this point, several members of my household had been diagnosed. We were all praying to spare me from this viral infection because we didn't know how it would impact my kidneys again.

As I cried at my desk, I began to think, "I Will Be Free," and I realized that freedom has to be an intentional posture. Freedom for me began to speak out in worship. Although I am in an unfortunate situation with unknown possibilities, I still serve Jesus Christ, who has commissioned me to complete a work. For me, freedom is acknowledging fear and disappointment in life but not allowing those things to paint a picture of death.

No one knows what tomorrow holds on this earth, but God does. So, let's not continue to waste moments that could be peaceful. Let's turn chaotic events into celebrations. Let's trust God even when our prayers are not always answered.

I sat at my desk and began thinking about you and what I would say to you today. I want to remind you that you will be free, and it starts with trusting God differently. Even when the odds are against you…Though he slay me, yet will I trust in him," (Job 13:15).

Today, you will not be afraid to become free, even at the cost of losing the old you, habits, ideologies, relationships, situationships, and dead weight. You will live with the intention of having freedom in your heart. It is easy to get caught up in feeling like life is not fair or to feel you do not understand why family, personal, and work relationships are so difficult to maintain. These things can become the weight, yoke of bondage, and hindrance in your life. Instead of being stuck focusing on the disparities we face in life and relationships, let's remind our hearts that God is just and always willing to help. In Him, we can find the freedom we need to move forward.

Life Is Not Fair

I used to think about so many regrets that don't solve a thing!! Revisiting regret makes you bitter, unlovable, unforgiving, and unwilling to trust those that God sends to help you. So, the next time you say life isn't fair or this isn't fair, think about the holes you are creating in your existence.

"Life Isn't Fair, Right?"

Of course, so many of us have said or thought this.

Before You Begin

So many of us have acted out, become someone different, and chosen to live a life of regret and defeat because we didn't get what we wanted. This is not to bash you for feeling how you feel. But it is a wake-up call not to stay here. Why? Every day, God gives you an opportunity to make new choices.

Yesterday, you may have made a decision that changed the trajectory of your life, but today is an opportunity to learn and grow with it. If I blame others I have learned nothing. If I blame myself, then I damage my ability to move forward in healing. But if I accept that I am flawed, human, and in desperate need of God's grace and direction; then I position myself to become better. I can now accept God's mercy and His ability to restore.

So, let's think about it. Life isn't fair, right? Or does life present an opportunity that is fair for you based upon the grace on your life? What if God has gifted you with the ability to overcome? What if God wants to put just enough strength within you to manage day-to-day so you lean on Him? What if God allows "life" or light afflictions to work out something greater on your behalf?

What if Life Isn't Fair, but God Is?

He is the Rock, his work is perfect: For all his ways are judgment: A God of truth and without iniquity, Just and right is he. Deuteronomy 32:4

Natalie Nichole
#brokenheartspeaks
10/09/2019

Prayer for Healthy Relationships

"Lord, allow me to attract people who have my best interest in mind. Allow me to meet people who challenge me but do not insult me. Allow me to be a recipient of love that covers faults and love that gracefully corrects. Allow me to meet people who apologize and not blame. Allow me to meet people drawn to my strengths and my weaknesses but not with the intent to exploit me. Allow me to build relationships built off love, trust, and respect.

Cover me from every snake-like spirit that is sent to distract, kill my confidence, and leave me wounded. Cover me from every jealous/envious spirit that sows words of discord and seeds of lies. Help me to accept that you love me. Help me to love myself, flaws and all. Help me to lean on you for guidance before seeking help from others. Protect my heart from attacks that revisit the pains of my past. Give me the wisdom needed to build healthy relationships of all sorts. Increase my discernment to see what is not seen and hear what is not heard. Build my confidence in you so that I can trust that this process is for my good.

In Jesus Name, Amen."

Prayer for Readers:

As we begin this journey, please read the following prayer to help guide your experience.

Desire to live for Christ
New Believer

"God, I recognize that my life is imperfect and that I need Jesus as my Lord and Savior to guide me through every moment of my life. I accept Jesus Christ as father, son, and comforter. I accept Jesus as the only perfect, blameless being who took on the penalty of sin for me. I honor His sacrifices that removed me from experiencing the penalty of death due to my sins. I can now have freedom and everlasting life in Christ because I accept His help to Live Again and become a disciple of His Word. In Jesus Name. Amen."

Desire to live differently for Christ
Believer

"God, I thank you for accepting me as your child. Thank you for the gift of salvation and the power you have given us to overcome this world. Empower me through your word with a new understanding of how to demonstrate my love and honor for you by choosing to live a life free from continual sin. God, I honor your sacrifice that removed me from experiencing the penalty of death due to my sins. I am thankful that I can ask for your help, and you will answer. I can continue to have different levels of freedom and everlasting life in you. In Jesus Name. Amen."

As you enter the I Will Be Free Journey, continue to remind yourself of God's immeasurable love and grace toward you. He will help you obtain freedom in Christ. Let's begin by preparing our hearts to address things that appear unfair and praying for God to direct our steps in choosing healthy relationships and surroundings to promote continual healing.

You know what's next. Let's #liveagain. You will be free!!

I WILL BE FREE!

Day 1

Day 1

Daily Checklist
- ☐ Read/study God's Word
- ☐ Repent
- ☐ Request God's Help
- ☐ Receive God's Love, Correction, and Instruction
- ☐ Re-Envision Yourself Free
- ☐ Remind yourself of God's Word and promises to you

I WILL BE FREE FROM REJECTION

Read: Psalm 94:14 and Psalm 51

For the Lord will not cast off his people, Neither will he forsake his inheritance. **Psalm 94:14**

Rejection… is embarrassing to talk about, especially in a world where the expectation is to be strong and continually allow offenses to roll off your back while pretending you are not hurt. Many ignore rejection and pretend to be OK when they are not. The acceptance of rejection looks like discrediting your God-given value and allowing the disapproval of others to stifle your faith in what God says about you.

Often, we see ourselves through the lens of another person's rejection instead of seeing ourselves through the lens of God's love and acceptance. The Word of God makes it very clear that God made men and women in His image and called them very good (Genesis 1:31). However, we

I WILL BE FREE FROM REJECTION

have allowed rejection, past mistakes, low self-esteem, and lack of acceptance of God's love to hinder us from honoring the good He has made in us.

I am not going to lie to you. Overcoming rejection is not easy, and it may come up in your life more often than you like. The goal is to learn how to depend on God's grace and rest in His love and acceptance during difficult seasons. God has made some promises to you. He promises to never leave you nor forsake you (Hebrews 13:5). The world may reject you, but God accepts you. He sees everything about you, yet He still wants you. Here is something you may not have heard recently.

You are wanted.
You are needed.
Your life has value.
You are <u>LOVED</u>.

Above all your flaws, insecurities, deficiencies, and other issues we don't have room to detail. You are still a part of God's original plan. He wants you to prosper and be in good health (3 John 1:2).

Today, you will make a declaration to reject the rejection and live in the love of God, who accepts every part of you (John 10:28).

Prayer

"Today, I reject the lies of my past and future. I will walk free of generational curses, fear, pain, covetousness, low self-esteem, people-pleasing, and all lies sent to rob me of my joy and future. God, I pray on today that your Word finds me and sets me free (John 8:36). I declare that I am beautifully and wonderfully made (Psalms 139:14). I am chosen, I am loved, and I am your child. I have help to overcome because you overcame the world. In Jesus Name Amen."

Affirmation

I will search out the good you made in me.

I WILL BE FREE FROM REJECTION
Notes

Day 2

Day 2

Daily Checklist
- ☐ Read/study God's Word
- ☐ Repent
- ☐ Request God's Help
- ☐ Receive God's Love, Correction, and Instruction
- ☐ Re-Envision Yourself Free
- ☐ Remind yourself of God's Word and promises to you

I WILL BE FREE FROM FEAR

Read: 2 Timothy 1:7; Psalm 55-56

For God hath not given us the spirit of fear; but of power, and of love, and of a sound mine. ***2 Timothy 1:7***

As humans, we all have a common denominator: fear. Some of us are afraid of bugs, heights, small spaces, and germs (I may or may not be talking about myself). Others are afraid to try new things, make new connections, or the big one: failure.

Fear is intended to keep us safe from harm. However sometimes we imagine things to be more harmful than they truly are, thus causing us to live paralyzed, gripped by fear. We find ourselves trying to plan our entire lives to avoid what we think is an avoidable mistake. The constant mind games we play with ourselves fuels fear, and fear drives our decision-making.

The spirit of fear does not resemble God's authority,

love, or sound mind. These negative emotions impact your rest cycle, alter the brain, invite hopelessness, and change the way you love yourself and others. Living in the spirit of fear causes you to feel unsafe all the time.

Fear is not the end of your story. As believers in Christ, we have many opportunities to run to Christ for safety, and He gives our hearts rest (Matthew 11: 28-30). When your heart is overwhelmed and feels unsafe, you can cry out to Jesus for help (Psalm 61:2-4). Fear is natural, but abiding by Christ is supernatural. I am not suggesting that you become 100% fearless; I am suggesting that you cast your fear on Him who is able to give you power, love, and a sound mind.

Prayer

"Today, I give the chronic spirit of fear to you. I come out of agreement with excessive worry, panic attacks, anxiety, and declare that my mind will rest. My heart will be at peace (John 14:27). I understand that no weapon formed against me shall prosper (Isaiah 54:17). Others trust in themselves, but I will trust in the name of the Lord, which is a strong tower. I choose to run to you knowing that I am safe (Proverbs 18:10-13). In Jesus Name. Amen"

Affirmation

I choose to not allow fear to rob me of daily rest.

Notes

Day 3

Day 3

Daily Checklist
- ☐ Read/study God's Word
- ☐ Repent
- ☐ Request God's Help
- ☐ Receive God's Love, Correction, and Instruction
- ☐ Re-Envision Yourself Free
- ☐ Remind yourself of God's Word and promises to you

I WILL BE FREE FROM SELF-SABOTAGE

Read: 2 Corinthians 10:5; Psalm 32

Casting down imaginations, and every high thing that exalteth itself against the knowledge of God, and bringing into captivity every thought to the obedience of Christ.
Corinthians 10:5

I recall countless times that I have talked myself out of something I really wanted to do. These conversations with myself stemmed from a place of rejection and fear. Self-sabotage is beyond dangerous as it creates patterns, perceptions, and imaginations that become an island of self-destructive thoughts. I remember telling myself I wasn't good enough. And before I knew it, year after year had gone by, and I was surrounded by a body of negative words.

I want to encourage you to not allow your inability to be perfect to create a partial reality that lies would support. The truth is you will always make mistakes, and you are not everyone's choice. The enemy uses this to condemn you to think that you have to be perfect, loved, and accepted by everyone. However, Romans 3:23 reminds us that no one is perfect and we all have sinned and fallen short.

But you are a friend of God (James 2:23). You are more than a conqueror (Romans 8:30). The areas in which you are weak and imperfect are perfectly created opportunities to help you find strength in Christ (2 Corinthians 12: 9-10).

Prayer

"Today, I pray that I learn to appreciate everything that has happened in my life, knowing that every situation has helped me to become stronger in my walk (Romans 8:28). I repent for allowing disappointments to create a system of beliefs that lacks faith and gratitude for your daily mercies. I will speak your word over my life and I trust that your word will be my guiding principles (Proverbs 3:5-6). Lord, I need your help to train my thoughts and create new patterns and perceptions. I throw away all old imaginations that make self-sabotage an idol in my life. In Jesus Name. Amen"

Affirmation

If I can capture my negative thoughts, then I can capture my future and hold it hostage.

Notes

Day 4

Day 4

Daily Checklist
- ☐ Read/study God's Word
- ☐ Repent
- ☐ Request God's Help
- ☐ Receive God's Love, Correction, and Instruction
- ☐ Re-Envision Yourself Free
- ☐ Remind yourself of God's Word and promises to you

I WILL BE FREE FROM UNFORGIVENESS

Read: Colossians 3:13; Psalm 31

Forbearing one another, and forgiving one another, if any man have a quarrel against any, even as Christ forgave you, so also do ye. **Colossians 3:13**

Many have heard this simple but complex message. "If you forgive, you will be forgiven, but if you do not forgive, you will not be forgiven" (Matthew 6:14-15). Reality check: nothing and I mean nothing, is simple about forgiveness, especially after being hurt. Our human nature wants others to acknowledge our pain. Our pride wants to share the pain with others.

It is this sense of entitlement that requires someone to apologize first before we even consider forgiving them. I remember pairing my lack of faith to forgive with words like this: "God knows me, so of course He knows I am not ready to let this hurt go." "I just need to vent. I am not talking about the person but the situation that hurt me." "I am just sharing my truth, and it is ok for me to not be ok."

You are right. It is okay not to be okay, but it is not okay to live in unforgiveness. Salvation through Christ was gifted to us through an unselfish act of unconditional love and forgiveness. Because we have an immeasurable amount of grace extended to us through Christ daily, we are required to extend the same level of grace to others daily.

Lastly, forgiveness does not overlook boundaries. It does not forget the wrong done to you. Instead, forgiveness is a conscious choice to teach your heart to be at peace with God and others. It chooses to love the unlovable, honor the dishonorable, and forgive the unforgivable.

Prayer

"Today, I pray to not rehearse the pain of unforgiveness. I confess that I have done things against my Lord and others deserving of unforgiveness. But I am thankful that I can accept forgiveness in Christ as He throws all my sins into a sea of forgetfulness. I understand I may not always forget the pain, but I declare that my mind is being transformed and becoming renewed to trust you. Today, I trust that my healing journey continues as I forgive others so that I can also be forgiven by you. In Jesus Name. Amen."

Affirmation

Forgiveness is my choice, and by faith, I will learn how to forgive the things I don't understand.

Notes

Day 5

Day 5

Daily Checklist
- ☐ Read/study God's Word
- ☐ Repent
- ☐ Request God's Help
- ☐ Receive God's Love, Correction, and Instruction
- ☐ Re-Envision Yourself Free
- ☐ Remind yourself of God's Word and promises to you

I WILL BE FREE FROM RESISTANCE

Read: James 4:7-10, Psalm 3

Submit yourselves therefore to God. Resist the devil, and he will flee from you. Draw nigh to God, and he will draw nigh to you... **James 4:7-8**

Life… always has and always will have uncertainties. Just like there are four seasons: spring, summer, fall, and winter; our lives can resemble aspects of the changing seasons without a known expiration date. If we are not careful, our hearts can build resistance to God's promises because our natural timeline and God's don't match. Sometimes, it becomes hard and even embarrassing to admit that, as believers in Christ, our faith has been resistant at times. But God is prepared for you, and He will not allow your faithless questions to cause you to fall (I Corinthians 10: 12-13).

We live with frustration on our tongues and hope-

I WILL BE FREE FROM RESISTANCE

lessness in the back of our minds. This resistance is an open door for the enemy to lie to us and keep us living in a place of discouragement. But the Word of God reminds us that if God be for us who can be against us (Romans 8:31).

The great thing about seasons are **they do change**. Sometimes there appears to be a delay but God's timing is perfecting something within you. Take time to remember that God is the potter, and we are the clay (Romans 9:19).

God is still forming us to be more like Him. God has power over your clay of life. The resistance of your thoughts doesn't dictate how the potter chooses to form you.

Prayer

"God, I repent for allowing my mind to wander into negative places. I repent for allowing my mouth to speak against your work in progress. I repent for being impatient, quick to anger, and quick to speak. Help me in the various seasons of my life to trust you despite what things look like (Hebrews 11:1).
God, I will remember that you are my shield (Psalms 3:3), and you will save me from thoughts that resist the power of your Word working in me. In Jesus Name, Amen."

Affirmation

As the clay is in the potter's hand, forming easily without resistance. I will remember that I am in your hands and will not resist you. Jeremiah 18:6

I WILL BE FREE FROM RESISTANCE

Notes

Day 6

Day 6

Daily Checklist
- ☐ Read/study God's Word
- ☐ Repent
- ☐ Request God's Help
- ☐ Receive God's Love, Correction, and Instruction
- ☐ Re-Envision Yourself Free
- ☐ Remind yourself of God's Word and promises to you

I WILL BE FREE FROM ANGER

Read: James 1:19-20, Psalm 34

Wherefore, my beloved brethen, let every man be swift to hear, slow to speak, slow to wrath: for the wrath of man worketh not the righteous of God. **James 1:19-20**

  I remember as a child that, my mother suffered a head injury as a result of an accidental fall. Sometimes, she would experience temporary moments of blindness. I noticed that the blindness would happen as a result of her emotional state, namely when she would become upset. Anger itself is a natural emotion and can not always be avoided. However, explosive anger has the potential to cause blindness in our lives when we react contrary to the fruit of the spirit.

  The Word of God encourages us to be angry and sin not (Ephesians 4:26). We can avoid some of the chaos that is created from our responses if we take time to acknowledge our anger and God at the same time (Proverbs 3:5-6). Yes, I said acknowledge our anger and God at the same time!!!

Jesus was tempted in every area, yet without sin. So he understands exactly how you feel and wants to help you at that very moment. He gave us himself. He is living inside of us and all we have to do is allow God's breath of life to get us back on track.

You can practice this by taking time to breathe in and out. Breathe in the peace of God and breathe out the frustrations in the moment. Explosive reactions can be a cycle that can be broken in your life. It begins with taking a moment to pause, slow down, and allow our emotions to come into alignment with the peace of God, which frees us from anger that causes us to sin.

Prayer

"Lord, save me from the anger that blinds me from giving and receiving your love. I repent from holding things in and allowing my emotions to attack my body. Teach me how to release my anger and frustrations to you. Teach me how to be slow to anger and swift to listen to you and your leading. I may not understand everything that happens around me, but I trust you with my life. I choose to walk in your principles. In Jesus Name, Amen"

Affirmation

I will create a Christ-centered system in my life instead of succumbing to my emotional responses, which are birthed from anger.

Notes

Day 7

Day 7

Daily Checklist
- ☐ Read/study God's Word
- ☐ Repent
- ☐ Request God's Help
- ☐ Receive God's Love, Correction, and Instruction
- ☐ Re-Envision Yourself Free
- ☐ Remind yourself of God's Word and promises to you

I WILL BE FREE FROM ACCUSATION

Read: Isaiah 54:17, Psalm 109

No weapon that is formed against thee shall prosper; and every tongue that shall rise against thee in judgment thou shalt condemn. This is the heritage of the servants of the Lord, and their righteousness is of me, saith the LORD.
Isaiah 54:17

In the justice system, you have heard of the phrase "innocent until proven guilty." But having faith in Christ, this is reversed; we are the guilty proven to be innocent due to His forgiveness of sins (Romans 4: 5-8). We are free from condemnation, and the Spirit of life in Christ has made us free from the law of sin and death (Romans 8:1).

As you continue to apply His Word and standards to your life, you will see new things shaping and molding you to reflect the mind of Christ. Your soul, old ways, and thought process are being purified when you accept and obey the Spirit of truth (I Peter 1:22). It is our responsibility to counteract those things spoken against you with God's word. You have authority in the Word of God to war against the accusations the enemy brings up. You also have to be careful not to accuse yourself.

Accusations are sometimes lies painted with a hint of truth to discourage you from moving forward. It may be true that a mistake was made, moral failure occurred, and you used to do things that you are no longer proud of. But the Word of God reminds you that in Christ, you are a new creature, and all old things are passed away (2 Corinthians 6:17).

Accusations seem true and can lead us to continue walking in condemnation. But today, you are free from condemnation and all accusations against your past and future. You are Christ's beloved, and you are His child, who will look brighter in the future.

Prayer

"Father, help me to see myself the way you see me. Your word reminds me that I am made in your image and likeness. Therefore I desire to speak well of myself and trust you to continually transform my thoughts. Father, I am your child; therefore, I know I have your power to overcome accusations of my past and future. I declare that I will walk in new freedom and cast down every vain imagination that exalts itself against the knowledge of God. In Jesus Name, Amen"

Affirmation

I will be free from the things that were said about me, even if it used to be true. I am now a new creation in Christ.

Notes

Day 8

Day 8

Daily Checklist
- ☐ Read/study God's Word
- ☐ Repent
- ☐ Request God's Help
- ☐ Receive God's Love, Correction, and Instruction
- ☐ Re-Envision Yourself Free
- ☐ Remind yourself of God's Word and promises to you

I WILL BE FREE FROM CONFUSION & CHAOS

Read: Jeremiah 3:25; Psalm 71

We lie down in our shame, and our confusion covered us: for we have sinned against the LORD our God, we and our fathers, from our youth even unto this day, and have not obeyed the voice of the Lord our God. ***Jeremiah 3:25***

If you had grandparents from the South, you may have heard this old saying, "You don't believe fat meat is greasy." This is usually something said after someone has provided instructions or guidance that was overlooked or ignored. The Word of God provides wisdom and perimeters on how we should interact with others and respond to events. But just like I didn't always listen to my grandparents, we don't always listen to God, as all have sinned and fallen short of the glory of God (Romans 3:23).

Sometimes, we don't know we are being disobedient; other times, we are willfully disobedient. This disobedience ushers in chaos, confusion, instability, and prevents us from making Godly decisions. Just think back to the Garden of Eden. God gave Adam one rule and one rule alone.

Yet, Adam wasn't able to keep the one commandment to avoid eating from the tree in the middle of the garden. Adam's disobedience ushered in confusion and chaos for generations. Unfortunately, confusion never operates alone. It creates new cycles of stagnation by making you afraid or angry and aids you in not trusting God.

But God is not the author of confusion, but of peace (I Corinthians 14:33). It is God's desire for you to have peace and the ability to make healthy decisions. This starts by repenting to God for the inability to follow His guidance. As we pray to God for His wisdom, understanding, and redirection when we don't get it right; God will provide a safety net of His grace and mercy to help us get back on track. As we ask for His wisdom, incline our ear to Him, He becomes our hiding place and strong habitation to overcome confusion and chaos (Psalm 71).

Prayer

"God, I come out of agreement with all confusion and chaos that has caused instability in my life. God, I will allow your Word to lead me and train me to become free from everything rooted in some form of trauma. I believe you to bring stability back to my mind, home, family, and everything related to me that brings you glory. In Jesus Name Amen."

Affirmation

I will seek you for guidance and solutions that align with your Word and will for my life.

Notes

Day 9

Day 9

Daily Checklist
- ☐ Read/study God's Word
- ☐ Repent
- ☐ Request God's Help
- ☐ Receive God's Love, Correction, and Instruction
- ☐ Re-Envision Yourself Free
- ☐ Remind yourself of God's Word and promises to you

I WILL BE FREE FROM GRIEF

Read: Isaiah 57:18; Psalm 34

I have seen his ways, and I will heal him: I will lead him also and restore comforts unto him and to his mourners.
Isaiah 57:18

Grief is a personalized emotional response to a loss of any kind and can often feel unbearable. The personal, intimate nature of each situation makes it very difficult to analyze the pain of others. As believers in Christ, when you are grieving, you may need a reminder that Christ understands your pain and that He is not penalizing you for being in pain.

Instead, Christ encourages you to give your concerns to Him (Matthew 11:27) and allow Him to comfort you in your time of need (Matthew 5:4). I wish I could tell you that you will never cry or lose someone or something important to you. What I can offer you is that as you walk

I WILL BE FREE FROM GRIEF

through any season of grief, Christ will be your strength, and He understands every tear. He understands the questions you may have, the disappointments you face, and the brokenness that is in your heart. He wants you to trust Him with your brokenness and allow Him to restore your joy again.

This journey of grief will not always be easy, and you may have unexpected emotions on a good day. Just know that God is nigh unto them who have a broken heart (Psalm 34:18). You do not have to endure this season of your life alone. Just as Christ has you on His mind, He will also put you on the hearts of others just so you can remember that you are loved and not alone.

Prayer

"God, today I trust you with my pain. Your word reminds me that you are close to the brokenhearted and therefore, I am thankful that I am not alone. God, I don't always understand the "why's" but I know you are my comfort, my help, and my hiding place. I know that when I am overwhelmed, I can cry out to you, and you will answer. God, I thank you in advance for giving me the strength to face each day and depend on your daily grace and strength. In Jesus Name. Amen"

Affirmation

I trust God to restore my joy as I grieve and heal.

Notes

Day 10

Day 10

Daily Checklist
- ☐ Read/study God's Word
- ☐ Repent
- ☐ Request God's Help
- ☐ Receive God's Love, Correction, and Instruction
- ☐ Re-Envision Yourself Free
- ☐ Remind yourself of God's Word and promises to you

I WILL BE FREE FROM IRRESPONSIBLE STEWARDSHIP

Read: Genesis 1: 28; Psalm 104

In Genesis during the creation, God blessed Adam and Eve and declared that they would be fruitful, multiply, replenish, and subdue the earth. **Genesis 1:28**

God has entrusted you with ownership, responsibility, and accountability. You were born to become a good steward over everything created by God in your life.

Biblical stewardship is an act of worship unto God and a response to His goodness. When you operate in biblical stewardship this takes into consideration that everything God gives you is a gift and worthy of multiplication. The blessing of the Lord, it maketh rich, and he addeth no sorrow with it (Proverbs 10:22).

If you have an uplifting personality, it is not for you to keep to yourself, but it is for you to share the goodness of Christ with others (Ephesians 2:8-9). Every God-given gift has a purpose and should be handled with care. As a result of practicing Godly stewardship in your life, you open yourself up to eternal rewards and a life that bears the fruit of God's goodness.

Life is a precious gift and as you are faithful over a few things, He will make you ruler over many things (Matthew 25:23).

Prayer

"God on today, I am thankful for the life you have given me and the opportunities that exist for me to create more. Help me to trust you to multiply your goodness in my life and in the lives of those I influence. Help me to depend on your methods for obtaining natural and spiritual rewards. In Jesus Name, Amen."

Affirmation

My life is a testament of God's goodness, and I am a gift to others.

Notes

Day 11

Day 11

Daily Checklist
- ☐ Read/study God's Word
- ☐ Repent
- ☐ Request God's Help
- ☐ Receive God's Love, Correction, and Instruction
- ☐ Re-Envision Yourself Free
- ☐ Remind yourself of God's Word and promises to you

I WILL BE FREE FROM SEXUAL SINS (Past, Current, Future)

Read: I Corinthians 6:12; Psalm 119:45-48

And such were some of you: but ye are washed, but ye are sanctified, but ye are justified in the name of the Lord Jesus, and by the Spirit of our God. ***I Corinthians 6:12***

    Because of my mother's sexual history, being a single parent of five children, and never being married, she never had high expectations for me in reference to sexual purity. In fact, her only request was that I would wait to have sex until after I graduated high school. As a result, I didn't understand my value, nor have any teaching about sexual ties or the institution of marriage. Often, sex is a taboo conversation due to its private nature, and many enter into sexual agreements unaware of the spiritual strongholds and consequences.

    I married at 20 years old. I did not fully understand that sex was designed for intimacy and connection in marriage. It wasn't just something to do that would please my husband, but when done in marriage without all the noise from pornography and past relationships, sex in marriage pleases God.

Now keep in mind that sexual purity can be obtained at any age. This is not just for those who have done "the do." This is a reminder that God can purify your thoughts and help you become disciplined in your body to overcome a sexually provocative culture. God wants to help us silence the noise of unmarried sexual desires that produce rotten fruit.

After my divorce, I had a new silent struggle as I never felt comfortable enough to talk about my sexual history or the need for deliverance from thoughts and actions that plagued me. How do I transition to not having any sex at all because I am no longer married?

After several years of having impure thoughts and actions, I had to create boundaries in my life that promoted healing. There were seasons in my life when I monitored conversations, music, and entertainment. I understood that I was not strong enough to fight sexual desires on my will alone. I needed God's help, plus personal boundaries. Can a man take fire in his bosom and his clothes not be burned (Proverbs 6:26)?

Therefore, I learned to discipline my thoughts and body by fasting. He that hath no rule over his own spirit is like a city that is broken down without walls (Proverbs 25:28). I surrounded myself with those who were also fighting for purity and looking for ways to break agreement with compromise. Let me be clear: all sex outside of marriage is a trap from the enemy. Culture creates a narrative that "safe sex," such as protected sex or masturbation, is ok, but it does not line up with God's plan.

You may have been told that you can choose what to do with your body and your feelings about sex. Culture says it's your body, it's your choice; just make sure to practice "safe sex." I learned the hard way that there is no such thing as "safe sex" when done outside of the will of God.

When sex is introduced outside of a marriage consecrated by Christ, it creates an ongoing feeling of shame, guilt, and feelings of defeat once we are introduced to what God really desires for us. God's intention for sex was to unify a married couple in mind, body, and soul. When sex is done haphazardly, we build connections with people who are not our spouse.

Many have fallen victim to a false doctrine of "safe sex." Feelings and hormones are real; however, feelings are not always true. When our feelings create a narrative that goes against God's purpose for our sexual desires, we need to maintain boundaries and ask for help from a trusted same-sex confident who is also living consecrated before Christ.

But despite your past or current state. God wants to remind you that no matter what decisions that have been made about your sexual desires. He can purify your thoughts and retrain you to accept His will for the original plan. Yes, you can start over again and create boundaries in your daily life to consecrate your sexual desires (2 Corinthians 5:17).

I WILL BE FREE FROM SEXUAL SINS (Past, Current, Future)

Being free from sexual sins takes consistent discipline and time. You can break generational curses. You can influence the lives of those you are assigned to impact, by teaching them God's original purpose for sex and striving for purity. As a former offender of this, I can attest that God makes everything new. We serve a God who redeems the time.

If you choose to repent, create boundaries, study God's purpose for your life, and discipline your sexual desires, God will provide a way of escape each and every time (I Corinthians 10:13). God doesn't throw us away because of our sins. Our sins should encourage us to find safety in Christ, knowing that His sacrifice removed the penalty of a natural death for our sins. Therefore, because of Christ's sacrifice, I can be free from these feelings of shame, guilt, and defeat. Are you up to the challenge?

Will you allow God to sustain you in your walk toward sexual freedom? Will you be free?

Prayer

"God, I come before You with a heart of repentance for the times I have allowed my emotions, hormones, and misunderstandings about your purpose to take precedence over You. I know I can receive Your forgiveness, and I seek a new level of healing in my mind and body. I declare that my body will be a living sacrifice to You. I choose to break free from the bonds of sexual sin and reject anything that seeks to hold my future hostage.

I trust that You will break every chain and fetter in my life. I submit myself to Christ, resisting the devil, knowing that sexual sin will flee from me. Teach me to establish healthy boundaries, give me the strength to say no, and guide me to the accountability I need for this lifestyle change. Help me to let go of old habits and create new, uplifting thoughts. I will not live in shame or guilt over past or future sins. I trust You to lead me toward sustainable purity.
In Jesus Name. Amen"

Affirmation

I CAN DO ALL THINGS THROUGH CHRIST WHO STRENGTHENS ME. I Will Be Free from sexual sins: past, current, and future.

I WILL BE FREE FROM SEXUAL SINS (Past, Current, Future)

Notes

Day 12

Day 12

Daily Checklist
- ☐ Read/study God's Word
- ☐ Repent
- ☐ Request God's Help
- ☐ Receive God's Love, Correction, and Instruction
- ☐ Re-Envision Yourself Free
- ☐ Remind yourself of God's Word and promises to you

I WILL BE FREE FROM SHAME

Read: Isaiah 61:7; Psalm 25

For your shame, ye shall have double; and for confusion, they shall rejoice in their portion: therefore in their land they shall possess double: everlasting joy shall be unto them. ***Isaiah 61:7***

Shame starts off feeling like a dirty word that can not be scrubbed from our soul or past. The incidents are replayed over and over. Rehearsed to perfection, just in case you need to prepare a counterargument. Shame is an invincible weight that makes your heart heavy as you sift through the judgment of others. Shame was overcome by Christ because the scriptures state, "Whosoever believeth on him shall not be ashamed" (Romans 10:11).

Although shame can be a heavy burden often rooted in past mistakes or perceived inadequacies, it is important to remember that shame does not define our worth in

Christ's eyes. "There is therefore no condemnation to them that are in Christ Jesus, who walk not after the flesh but after the Spirit" (Romans 8:1). You overcome shame by submitting your past, current, and future to Christ.

Constant shame disregards Christ as the forgiver of all things. It doesn't matter what was done because in Christ, you are now scrubbed clean. "If we confess our sins, he is faithful and just to forgive us of our sins, and to cleanse us from all unrighteousness (I John 1:9)."

Prayer

"God, forgive me for holding my future hostage by replaying the errors of my past. I know that you love me. Help me to receive your love and forgiveness. I desire to walk free from shame and condemnation and stand strong, knowing that I am your child and you are my father. In Jesus Name. Amen."

Affirmation

I am loved and forgiven by God. My worth was established by the sacrifice Christ made for me.

Notes

Day 13

Day 13

Daily Checklist
- ☐ Read/study God's Word
- ☐ Repent
- ☐ Request God's Help
- ☐ Receive God's Love, Correction, and Instruction
- ☐ Re-Envision Yourself Free
- ☐ Remind yourself of God's Word and promises to you

I WILL BE FREE FROM BITTERNESS

Read: Hebrews 12:14-15, Psalm 73

"Follow peace with all men, and holiness, without which no man shall see the Lord: looking diligently lest any man fail of the grace of God; lest any root of bitterness springing up trouble you, and thereby many be defiled. **Hebrews 12:14-15**

    I can admit that there were seasons in my life where I was never satisfied. Things were just merely "ok." I would pride myself on being realistic, full of wisdom, and having discernment. I had no clue that my heart was critically defiled by the disappointments of life. All the while, I was discrediting the good things happening in my life and creating distance between good people in my life.

    I remember I started attending a church and everyone would say I love you after just meeting me. This had me so confused and I had many questions. "How can someone love me that doesn't know anything about me?" What I didn't understand at the time was I was so bitter from lingering anger at life being unfair. I was blinded by the pain of life events that I had absolutely no control over.

Has that ever happened to you? You weren't the one that caused the abuse to happen. You don't understand why someone special had to die? You never understood why you were teased, bullied, rejected, talked about, or the black sheep of the family.

Unresolved anger constantly seeps in early on and builds a bridge to bitterness because we often secretly desire to see others hurt when we hurt. But God reminds us that, "Vengeance is mine. I will repay saith the Lord" (Romans 12:19).

The pain is real. Your response to pain is valid, and you are human. God never intended us to carry these heavy burdens. But now that sin nature has entered the earth and our lives, we find our spiritual beings at war with the sin nature (James 4:17).

You are not responsible for the choices of others or the hurt done to you. You have a responsibility to heal, to choose to move forward– one day at a time. I am not going to lie to you; deep hurt takes time to heal, but the time must be intentionally spent. My ask of you today is to introduce Jesus to your pain. As you let Christ in, the crisis will start to diminish, and He will introduce you to a life filled with abundance (John 10:10).

Prayer

"God, I first repent for allowing bitterness to shape my actions and reactions to your goodness. I am thankful for my ability to move forward in your abundance of peace in my life. Today Father, I ask for your help. Help my unbelief as I battle the many questions I have in my head. Help me to release all my pain to you and look to you for daily guidance on living free in you. In Jesus Name. Amen"

Affirmation

Pain is not the marker of my destiny. Pain is merely a part of my history that is being restored by God's love and grace.

Notes

Day 14

Day 14

Daily Checklist
- ☐ Read/study God's Word
- ☐ Repent
- ☐ Request God's Help
- ☐ Receive God's Love, Correction, and Instruction
- ☐ Re-Envision Yourself Free
- ☐ Remind yourself of God's Word and promises to you

I WILL BE FREE FROM NEGATIVE WORDS

Read: Ephesians 4:29; Psalm 119:9-16

Let no corrupt communication proceed out of your mouth, but that which is good to the use of edifying, that it may minister grace unto the hearers. ***Ephesians 4:29***

You have probably heard the old saying, "If you don't have anything nice to say, don't say anything at all." I challenge you to take that same approach to yourself. God created you with a greater purpose in mind.

A part of that purpose is for your life to bring Him glory. God rejoices when your Words are used to heal as opposed to being used to destroy. "Death and life are in the power of the tongue: and they that love it shall eat the fruit thereof" (Proverbs 18:21).

You serve an all-powerful God who used His words to formulate everything that is needed. Not only did God

I WILL BE FREE FROM NEGATIVE WORDS

Himself use words to create life, God is the living Word of our lives and He is the source of all life (John 1:1). In honor of God being the Word, our words should demonstrate reverence, carefulness, and wisdom.

Your words are more powerful than you realize. The words you choose have the potential to heal or destroy. Most importantly, your words are not just for you. They become seeds for your future and those connected to you.

I encourage you today to choose words that bring forth life and are shaped by the Living Word. Take a moment to practice restraint with your words and allow God to create a different level of maturity and gentleness. Psalm 34:13 says, "Keep thy tongue from evil And thy lips from speaking guile."

Prayer

"God, please forgive me for using my words to sow seeds of discord in my life and the lives of others. Lord, empower me to depend on your holy spirit and guiding principles to choose my words wisely. I admit that I fall short in this area, and I am open to allowing your Word to fill my mouth and transform my heart. In Jesus Name, Amen."

Affirmation

I choose to select words that will love myself and others back to life.

Notes

Day 15

Day 15

Daily Checklist
- ☐ Read/study God's Word
- ☐ Repent
- ☐ Request God's Help
- ☐ Receive God's Love, Correction, and Instruction
- ☐ Re-Envision Yourself Free
- ☐ Remind yourself of God's Word and promises to you

I WILL BE FREE FROM PRIDE

Read: Romans 3:23, Romans 12:3, Psalm 131

For all have sinned, and come short of the glory of God.
Romans 3:23

As a teenager, I was often the topic of harsh discussions: often bullied, talked about, and mishandled for various reasons. Some judged me because they judged my mother's lifestyle of being a single mother of five children. As a result of feeling mishandled, deeply hurt, and wanting acceptance of others.

I found myself mixing religion with my emotional pain in hopes that God was going to punish everyone who bullied me. I often quoted Romans 12:3:

> *"For I say, through the grace given unto me, to every man that is among you, not to think of himself more highly than he ought to think, but*

to think soberly, according as God hath dealt to every man the measure of faith."

Pride is much more widespread than we realize. It's so easy to recognize when someone is bragging, arrogant, compulsive, etc. But it is very difficult to see it within ourselves when we devalue our accomplishments more than we spend time with God. Pride looks like self-sabotage. Your thoughts become an idol place of worship for everything wrong with you. Pride has a way of sneaking into each of our hearts and pitching a tent unbeknownst to us. Pride promotes becoming unteachable, argumentative, confrontational, or embarrassed to speak up due to self-condemnation.

We all are in need of Jesus Christ as our Savior because His written word gives us tools to walk towards freedom only found in Him. Stand fast therefore in the liberty wherewith Christ hath made us free, and be not entangled again with the yoke of bondage (Galatians 5:1). Pride is a yoke of bondage but when we accept Christ, we now have the ability to give Him everything that hurts us and weighs us down.

We can cry out to Abba Father, and He will tend to the cry of His children.

Be encouraged. We all have sinned and fallen short of God's glory. But that is why Christ came. He came to set us free from the captivities that remain in our hearts and minds. It's not an easy task for men, but all things are possible with God (Matthew 19:26).

Prayer

"God, I thank you that all my sins are already forgiven. Help me to apply your word to my heart daily. I repent for not being grateful and graceful to others. Let your word be a lamp unto my feet and a light unto my path (Psalms 119:105). God, I trust you to help me with any area of my heart that lives in self-sabotage, self-condemnation, self-demotion, self-exaltation, self-promotion, and self-justification. God, I come out of agreement with being argumentative, boastful, condescending, and having false humility. I take on your character to have a renewed mind and transformed heart. In Jesus' Name, Amen."

Affirmation

I will look to Christ for strategies to overcome the sin in my heart.

Notes

Day 16

Day 16

Daily Checklist
- ☐ Read/study God's Word
- ☐ Repent
- ☐ Request God's Help
- ☐ Receive God's Love, Correction, and Instruction
- ☐ Re-Envision Yourself Free
- ☐ Remind yourself of God's Word and promises to you

I WILL BE FREE FROM A BROKEN HEART

Read: Psalm 147:3, Psalm 23

He healeth the broken in heart, and bindeth up their wounds. ***Psalm 147:3***

Have you ever dropped a glass jar and noticed how it shatters into bits and pieces everywhere? Once the shattering has occurred, it is impossible to try to put the item back together. Usually, there are pieces scattered everywhere, and if you are anything like me, you may find pieces of glass in other areas of the house days or weeks later.

Unfortunately, your heart can also experience a great amount of pain to the point that it feels shattered or broken like pieces of you are everywhere. A broken heart is a natural and spiritual occurrence. In the medical world, it is referred to as broken heart syndrome. This condition is brought on by stressful situations, but with time, it can be healed.

I WILL BE FREE FROM A BROKEN HEART

A broken heart can result from mourning caused by a loss of relationships, materials/property, financial security, employment, opportunities, major transitions, or unmet expectations. These are a few things that can weigh heavily on our hearts and cause a break in our mental processing and peace of mind.

As humans, our natural responses at times can reflect disappointment. We have to choose to allow the disappointments to be temporary. First thing first, remember that mourning does not make you less spiritual or loved by God. In fact, He understands everything you are going through as Jesus also experienced loss as the bible recounts Jesus wept in John 11:35 after finding out that Lazarus, his friend had died.

In our moments of disappointment, we can choose to ask for help or live in constant pain without the option of receiving strength from Jesus. God wants to give you an expected end. He wants us to call out to Him, to pray, and He will hear us. Not only will God hear you but the word reminds us that he will seek you and find you (Jeremiah 29:11-14).

There may be seasons in your life where it feels like you can't find God. I want to encourage you that you never have to find God, just merely call out to Him and He will come find you and restore you. Our hearts can be healed when we take the time to share the shattered pieces with God.

Prayer

*"I thank you for your word that heals and binds up the brokenhearted. Help me to come out of agreement with things that have settled in my heart and caused my heart to be scattered. God, I know I can cry out to you for help,
and your word reminds me that you will answer. God, I thank you that this brokenness is temporary, and I trust you for my expected end of thoughts of peace. In Jesus' Name, Amen."*

Affirmation

I acknowledge my pain, and I give myself permission to heal because Christ is my healer.

Notes

Day 17

Day 17

Daily Checklist
- ☐ Read/study God's Word
- ☐ Repent
- ☐ Request God's Help
- ☐ Receive God's Love, Correction, and Instruction
- ☐ Re-Envision Yourself Free
- ☐ Remind yourself of God's Word and promises to you

I WILL BE FREE FROM THE BONDAGE OF SICKNESS, DISEASE, AND INFIRMITY

Read: II Corinthians 12:9, Psalm 41

And he said unto me, My grace is sufficient for thee: for my strength is made perfect in weakness. Most gladly therefore will I rather glory in my infirmities, that the power of Christ may rest upon me. ***II Corinthians 12:9***

Having a physical or emotional diagnosis of any kind can be very challenging, difficult to understand, and, at times, even frightening. Sickness exists because we live in an imperfect world due to sin. Once sin entered due to the choices of man, everything was subject to be impacted, including your health.

Even in the midst of sickness, it is imperative to understand that God is sovereign. He is the same yesterday, today, and forever (Hebrews 13:8). As believers in Christ, we trust that God's will is sovereign in our lives. So when we are faced with issues, we trust God for His help. God wants us to find safety in Him and not allow the reports to rule our faith (Isaiah 53:1). Today, I encourage you to look for goodness in your day, celebrate your progress, and ask God to strengthen your faith to understand that God is still in control of your life.

I've learned through my own medical diagnosis that God's timetable looks nothing like my own. The more I worry about my health, the less progress I make on improving my health. Instead, I have learned to trust God's process, listen to the wisdom of medical professionals, and take an active approach in my own healing process.

You have heard, "As man thinketh, so is he." It is imperative to think about God's healing in your mind and body. As you go through your process of healing, be encouraged. Do not compare your healing journey to anyone else. Instead, continue to trust God, praise God, and expect God's continual healing in your life.

"Bless the Lord, O my soul, And forget not all his benefits. Who forgiveth all thine iniquities; Who healeth all thy diseases; Who redeemeth thy life from destruction (Psalm 103: 1-4)."

I encourage you to trust God and take Him at His word as healer. Live a life demonstrating that you have become a good steward over your body and emotions. Psalm 41 offers a comforting reminder that God is with us during our times of sickness. He sustains us, bringing hope and healing. Each day is filled with brand new mercies and opportunities to live in God's grace and healing for your mind and body.

Prayer

"God, I trust you with my emotional, spiritual, and physical health. Give me wisdom and insight on how to better take care of my body so I can accomplish your will in the earth. God, help me depend on you as the first responder in my life. Help me to trust your timing and continue to grow strong in my faith, knowing that you will not fail me. In Jesus Name, Amen."

Affirmation

I will not allow sickness in my life or the lives of others to rob me of my faith. Your grace is sufficient for me.

Notes

Day 18

Day 18

Daily Checklist
- ☐ Read/study God's Word
- ☐ Repent
- ☐ Request God's Help
- ☐ Receive God's Love, Correction, and Instruction
- ☐ Re-Envision Yourself Free
- ☐ Remind yourself of God's Word and promises to you

I WILL BE FREE FROM DISTRACTIONS

Read: Romans 12:2, Psalm 86

And be not conformed to this world: but be ye transformed by the renewing of your mind, that ye may prove what is that good, and acceptable, and perfect, will of God.
Romans 12:2

Distractions can be people, places, or things that rob your attention from things that require your focus or a disciplined "yes" to Christ. One of my good friends always says, "If you say yes to one thing, then you are saying no to something else."

In Christ, we are becoming a new creature daily and this requires intentionality to identify those things in your daily behavior that diverts attention from a desired area of focus that brings God glory. Ask yourself, what things can you accomplish in a day if you didn't do something else?

I WILL BE FREE FROM DISTRACTIONS

Many distractions can be identified in your thinking about the future and the past.

Thinking ahead often creates obstacles in creating solutions in search of a problem. You become less engaged with the immediate needs of the day because plans are being created out of fear and insecurity to secure tomorrow. The Word of God reminds us that planning for our future out of fear is not our job. "Take therefore no thought for the morrow: for the morrow shall take thought for the things of itself" (Matthew 6:34).

Looking back is another culprit as it creates an imbalance in your natural and spiritual life. "Let thine eyes look right on, And let thine eyelids look straight before thee (Proverbs 4:25)." Keeping your eyes fixed on Jesus makes it easier to create forward movement with steps that please God.

God wants you to remember to look at Him as the author and finisher of your faith. You will overcome distractions by depending on God daily to empower you to make choices that demonstrate discipline. God is perpetual and desires for us to move forward (Luke 9:62) instead of living in the past.

You must train your day to include God and make room for Him. This enables you to limit some of the distractions by starting the day with prayer for wisdom, guidance, and discernment.

Prayer

"God, this is the day you have made, and I will rejoice and be glad in it. God, I need your help to create stability in my thoughts and actions. Each day, I desire to create healthy habits that create steps that enable me to become productive. God, increase my wisdom, guidance, discernment, and discipline to live a life that overcomes distractions. I can do all things through Christ which strengthens me (Philippians 4:13). In Jesus Name, Amen."

Affirmation

I will depend on Christ as the stabilizer of my thoughts and actions to produce forward movement in my life.

Notes

Day 19

Day 19

Daily Checklist
- ☐ Read/study God's Word
- ☐ Repent
- ☐ Request God's Help
- ☐ Receive God's Love, Correction, and Instruction
- ☐ Re-Envision Yourself Free
- ☐ Remind yourself of God's Word and promises to you

I WILL BE FREE FROM IMPATIENCE

Read: Ecclesiastes 7:8-9, Psalm 27

Better is the end of a thing than the beginning thereof: and the patient in spirit is better than the proud spirit. ***Ecclesiastes 7:8***

This scripture encourages us to be ok with finishing instead of rushing to be recognized for our accomplishments. We have to consistently evaluate our hearts and motives to ensure that pride is not the motivator in completing a task. We have to allow God to receive the glory in our waiting season. Waiting is not always welcomed, especially in a culture where things are readily accessible.

While writing this devotional, I created a strict timeline in hopes of finally finishing. However, due to life circumstances and, at times, writer's block, the timeline continued to grow. This uncertainty of not meeting "**<u>my scheduled deadline</u>**" started to create anxiety.

I WILL BE FREE FROM IMPATIENCE

I bet you can recall a time when you wanted to start or complete a task on a specific timeline. Oftentimes, our expectations meet an interference. As a result, you feel the need to rush or accomplish a task quickly. But our life timeline might not meet the timeline of God. A man's heart deviseth his way; but the Lord directed his steps (Proverbs 16:9).

God is so gracious; He consistently gives you the freedom to choose. You can choose to trust His timing and learn to accept his timelines. "Trust in the Lord with all thine heart; And lean not unto thine own understanding. In all thy ways acknowledge him, And he shall direct thy paths" (Proverbs 3:5-6).

In times of uncertainty, you may feel the need to rush or make a quick decision to finish a task. Consider taking time to pause and relax your timelines as you depend on God to provide additional guidance to complete the next steps.

Prayer

"God, I need your help to teach me to wait on you. As I wait on you, I pray that I gain the courage to choose you instead of choosing my own desires. Your word reminds me that my heart will be strengthened when I wait on you (Psalm 27:14). God, I repent for all the times I moved without considering what you wanted for me. I commit to taking time to ask for your guidance and wait on your instructions, in Jesus' Name, Amen."

Affirmation

I will give myself permission to pause to trust God for His help.

Notes

Day 20

Day 20

Daily Checklist
- ☐ Read/study God's Word
- ☐ Repent
- ☐ Request God's Help
- ☐ Receive God's Love, Correction, and Instruction
- ☐ Re-Envision Yourself Free
- ☐ Remind yourself of God's Word and promises to you

I WILL BE FREE FROM LAZINESS

Read: Genesis 1:28, Psalm 90:17

And God blessed them, and God said unto them, Be fruitful, and multiply, and replenish the earth, and subdue it: and have dominion over the fish of the sea, and over the fowl of the air, and over every living thing that moveth upon the earth. **Genesis 1:28**

The Word of God in Genesis calls you to produce, bear fruit, and influence Godly character in your surroundings. The pursuit of overcoming laziness involves cultivating a mindset that embraces productivity and intentionality. It's essential to recognize that taking breaks or addressing physical and mental health issues is not the same as laziness. Laziness, in this context, might be seen as a lack of willingness to use one's gifts and opportunities to their fullest potential.

Laziness as believers of Christ is an attack on God's

character living within you because God desires for you to have an excellent spirit that demonstrates influence. Laziness is the pulling away from God's power to do the work He has instructed you to do. "Not slothful in business, fervent in spirit, serving the Lord; rejoicing in hope, patient in tribulation, continuing instant in prayer, distributing to the necessity of saints, given to hospitality" (Romans 12:11-13).

Developing a productive mentality aligns with a commitment to excellence. It allows us to reflect God's character by striving to make a positive impact and demonstrate influence in our actions. Today, be encouraged, knowing that your life has great purpose and potential. Staying focused and open to God's leading and correction will help you overcome obstacles and distractions that can derail your progress.

Keep moving forward with confidence and determination, knowing that you're supported in your journey. Being confident of this very thing, that He who hath begun a good work in you will perform it until the Day of Jesus Christ (Philippians 1:5).

Prayer

"Today, God I thank you for your grace that extends me brand new mercies. Help me to allow your Word to search me and help me to make Godly choices that demonstrate your power in my life. I trust you to break alignment with words spoken over my life that impact my ability to work and move forward. Help me to create an influence in my life that leads others to Christ. God, as I read and study your word, guide me to the tools and resources needed to help me overcome laziness in my life. In Jesus Name Amen."

Affirmation

I will remember that I was created with your purpose to multiply the knowledge and love of Christ in the earth. I will multiply a God centered life.

Notes

Day 21

Day 21

Daily Checklist
- ☐ Read/study God's Word
- ☐ Repent
- ☐ Request God's Help
- ☐ Receive God's Love, Correction, and Instruction
- ☐ Re-Envision Yourself Free
- ☐ Remind yourself of God's Word and promises to you

I WILL BE FREE FROM ME

Read: Galatians 5:1; Psalm 118

Stand fast therefore in the liberty wherewith Christ hath made us free, and be not entangled again with the yoke of bondage. **Galatians 5:1**

Freedom is the ability to break free from the power of sin and live as God intended. Through Christ, we are liberated from the penalty of sin and its effects on our mind, body, and spirit. His sacrifice grants us access to the Holy Spirit's guidance and support.

To truly embrace this freedom, we must first acknowledge our flaws and recognize our need for a Savior. Eliminate excuses that keep you from living up to God's standards. Take time to reflect on areas where you need to surrender to Him, understanding that your journey may differ from others.

Incorporate self-reflection, prayer, and applied learning into your healing process. Seek out mature believers who can help hold you accountable as you pursue your goals. Allow the Word of God to transform you into a mature follower of Christ, receptive to His correction.

Remember, healing is a continual process, and we will always rely on God's help. Your ongoing commitment to Him will lead to deep, lasting change. Consider setting specific goals for your reflection and prayer time to deepen this journey. Identify areas where you feel God is prompting change, and be open to His guidance, even if it feels uncomfortable. Surround yourself with mature believers who can provide accountability and support as you navigate this process.

Remember, healing and deliverance are ongoing. Embrace the journey, and trust that you are becoming more aligned with God's purpose for your life with each step. Make intentional space for God, and let Him work in your heart and mind. Your commitment to this process will lead to profound transformation over time.

Prayer

"God, I thank you for your love and grace. I desire to live a life that does not take advantage of your grace, but instead, I live disciplined for you. Help me to embrace that you created me to live out loud and on purpose for you. God, your Word reminds me that when I am weak, then you are strong. Today, I stand on your strength as I commit to live a journey that reminds me of who I am in you. In Jesus Name, Amen."

Affirmation

I WILL BE FREE!!

Notes

Next Steps!

Next Steps!

Thank you for completing the **I Will Be Free 21-Day Challenge!**

I'm truly excited that you chose to participate and allowed Love That Saves ministry to be part of your journey. This moment is a celebration of your intentional decision to seek God for your freedom. Continue to lean on trusted friends, family, spiritual counselors, or your Pastor for support. Remember, you can revisit this book to reflect on the scriptures, prayers, and affirmations as you embrace your healing.

This resource is just one of many available to you. I encourage you to join our Live Again FB Community or YouTube Channel for fellowship, prayer, and deeper exploration of God's purpose for your life.

I look forward to hearing your testimonies from the I Will Be Free Challenge. You can submit them to lovethatsavesyou@gmail.com.

As always,

Pray Again
Love Again
Live Again

YOU WILL BE FREE

Join The Live Again Facebook Community

Subscribe to Live Again YouTube

Listen to the I Will Be Free Audio Recordings on YouTube
@LiveAgain21
01/11-2024-01/31-2024

Purchase Live Again 21-Day Prayer and Fasting Devotional

About the Author

Natalie Nichole, a native of Gary, IN, is the eldest of five children raised by a strong single mother who instilled the value of perseverance. A passionate minister, devoted mother, and loving wife, she has been married to Bobby Washington Jr. for two years, and together they nurture a blended family of seven children.

Natalie dedicates her life to sharing the transformative power of faith through everyday experiences. Her first book, Live Again: Putting Broken Hearts Back Together Again, resonated with readers seeking encouragement and spiritual growth. She continues this journey with her second book in the Love That Saves devotional series, I Will Be Free: My Declaration to Continual Self-Deliverance. This 21-day journey invites readers to reflect, pray, and grow, drawing from her own experiences as a woman of faith.

When she's not writing or ministering, Natalie enjoys quality time with her family, exploring nature, and engaging in community service. She believes that faith is the foundation of life and aims to create a living legacy that empowers others to break generational curses and embrace abundance. Her mantra—"Pray Again, Love Again, Live Again"—reflects her commitment to living in Christ each day. Join Natalie Nichole as she guides you through this devotional journey, encouraging you to grow in faith, embrace your freedom in Christ, and experience the abundant life God promises.

SCAN ME

Call or Text:
770-240-0089 Press Extension 1
Web: KLEpub.com
Email Services@klepub.com

It's time to start and finish YOUR Story!

KLE Publishing specializes in helping people become authors. In as little as 15 to 90 days, we can help you develop your books and e-books and publish to 39,000 outlets! We also offer audiobook services.

Write, Edit, Format, Publish
We can help from
Start to Finish.

Explore and learn more about published authors affiliated with KLE.

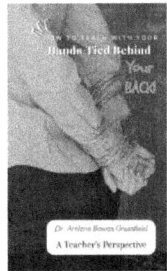

KLEPub.com

I Will Be FREE
My Declaration to Continual Self-Deliverance

I Will Be Free, the second book in the Love That Saves series, is transformative 21-day devotional inviting readers to explore an release the areas in their lives that limit spiritual freedom. emphasizes the power of daily prayer, transparency, an intentional habit-building to promote both spiritual growth and deeper acceptance of Christ's liberating grace. Anchored Galatians 5:1, which calls believers to stand firm in the freedo Christ provides, this devotional encourages readers to let go past burdens that threaten to hinder their progress. Throug practical insights and affirmations, *I Will Be Free* guides reade toward healing and ongoing self- deliverance, underscoring th true freedom is a daily commitment. Readers are empowered t cultivate a disciplined relationship with God, ultimatel embracing the fullness of their freedom in Christ.

Natalie Nichole, a native of Gary, IN, is the eldest of five children raised by a strong single mother who instilled the value of perseverance. A devoted mother, and loving wife, and together they nurture a blended family of seven children. Through prayer, love, and intentional living Natalie aims to cultivate meaningful connections and experiences in her life and the lives of those around her.

ISBN 978-1-9-4506663-4

9 781945 066634

www.ingramcontent.com/pod-product-compliance
Lightning Source LLC
Chambersburg PA
CBHW070103080526
44586CB00013B/1174